Staying Healthy, Safe and Well!

By Carmel Reilly

Pearson Australia
(a division of Pearson Australia Group Pty Ltd)
707 Collins Street, Melbourne, Victoria 3008
PO Box 23360, Melbourne, Victoria 8012
www.pearson.com.au

First published 2014 by Pearson Australia
2020 2019 2018 2017
10 9 8 7 6 5 4 3 2 1

Publisher: Kieren Noonan
Project Manager: Michelle Thomas
Editor: Margaret Trudgeon
Cover & Series Designers: Jenny Grigg and Anne Donald
Designer: Norma van Rees
Copyright & Pictures Editor: Katy Murenu
Mac Operator: Rob Curulli
Illustrator: Fiona Lee
Printed in Australia by the SOS Print + Media Group

ISBN 978 1 4860 0848 3
Pearson Australia Group Pty Ltd ABN 40 004 245 943

Acknowledgements
We would like to thank the following for permission to reproduce copyright material.
The following abbreviations are used in this list: t = top, b = bottom, l = left, r = right, c = centre.

Alamy: Andrew Fox, p. 10c; Radius Images, p. 16l.
Fotolia: pp. cover, 8br, 14b, 18, 19t, 20, 21, back cover.
Shutterstock: pp. 1, 3, 4, 5, 6(all), 7(all), 8cr, 8bl, 9(all), 10t, 11, 14t, 15(all), 16r, 19br, 17, 22.

Every effort has been made to trace and acknowledge copyright. However, should any infringement have occurred, the publishers tender their apologies and invite copyright owners to contact them.

Disclaimer
Some of the images used in *Staying Healthy, Safe and Well!* might have associations with deceased Indigenous Australians. Please be aware that these images might cause sadness or distress in Aboriginal or Torres Strait Islander communities.

Contents

Healthy living

Being healthy and feeling good is the best thing in the world. But how good we feel comes down to how we look after ourselves. Eating well and getting enough exercise will help us to stay fresh and energetic. It will also keep us at a healthy weight and protect us from diseases. We can also stay well by making sure we keep safe from harm and harmful **substances**.

A part of growing up is learning how to look after yourself. Knowing how to make the best choices will help to keep you healthy and safe as you grow and develop.

LET'S FIND OUT

- **Why are healthy food choices important?**
- **What does exercise do for us?**
- **Why is it important to know about the environment around us?**
- **Why do we need to be aware of the people around us?**
- **What are some of the ways different drugs can affect us?**

Eating healthy food is one way of staying healthy.

Fuel up!

Cars need fuel to make them move, and so do our bodies. But instead of petrol, we humans need food and water to keep us going. Just as cars need good-quality petrol to run at their best, we need good-quality food. The better the food we eat, the better we feel, and the more energy we have.

Eating the right stuff

Everything your body needs can be found in these five food groups:

- vegetables and legumes
- fruit
- grains (bread, cereals, rice, pasta, noodles)
- milk, yoghurt, cheese
- meat, fish, poultry, eggs, nuts and legumes.

This picture shows us how much we should be eating from each food group each day. The right balance of the best foods will make us feel great. Most of what we eat should be plant-based foods, like breads, vegetables and fruit. Animal-based foods, like milk and meat, should make up less than a quarter of our food.

Healthy-eating plate containing the five food groups we should eat from each day

Did you know?

Everyone should try to eat between two and nine serves (½ cup equals one serve) of vegetables each day, and one to five pieces of fruit.

What's on your plate?

Between them, the foods on the healthy-eating plate provide all the **nutrients** our bodies need to live and grow. They include **carbohydrates** to give us energy, **protein** to help us grow, and **vitamins** and **minerals** to keep us healthy and well. Eating a wide range of foods every week will give you a range of nutrients in different amounts, giving you the best fuel to keep you on the go.

Chips, cakes, sweets and softdrinks are not shown because they do not contain many healthy nutrients. They also contain a lot of sugar, salt or fat, which can make us put on weight and don't give us good, lasting energy. This doesn't mean we can't eat these things at all – just not too much or too often.

Red meat – protein, vitamin B_{12} for the brain and nervous system, iron for muscles and growth

Carrots – carbohydrates, vitamin A for the eyes and the immune system

Wholegrain wheat bread – carbohydrates, vitamins and minerals for growth and repair

Nutrients found in red meat, carrots and wholegrain bread

You can choose

Compare what you eat each day to the healthy-eating plate. Perhaps you already eat lots of fresh vegetables and fruit. But what if you don't?

It's easy to add healthy foods into your meals and snacks. A piece of fruit with breakfast and another as a snack for morning or afternoon tea is all you need to get the right amount of fruit. Tuck some lettuce or tomato into your sandwich at lunchtime, and make some interesting salads with cucumber, carrots or sprouts to go with dinner.

Healthy eating tips

- Eat the fresh food first, so you'll have less room for empty junk!
- Choose fresh fruit and vegetables as between-meal snacks
- Cut back on foods that are full of fat, sugar and salt. (Read food labels on packaged foods to see what is in them.)
- Make as much of your own food as possible, so you know exactly what goes into it.

Bought hamburger

Homemade hamburger

Make it yourself!

There are many tasty and healthy snacks that you can make yourself. Here is a snack that can be made quickly and easily and tastes great. You can also serve this with home-made nachos or tacos for lunch or dinner.

Guacamole with vegetable sticks

(Serves 2 people)

* You will need an adult to cut the avocado in half and cut the vegetables into sticks.

Ingredients:

1 large avocado

2–3 tablespoons of lemon or lime juice

1 small clove garlic crushed

1 tablespoon of sweet chilli sauce

¼ teaspoon salt

1 carrot cut into sticks

1 stalk of celery cut into sticks

Process:

1. Mash the avocado in a bowl.
2. Add the juice, garlic, sweet chilli sauce and salt and mix together.
3. Check for taste and add more sauce, salt or juice if needed.
4. Serve with carrot and celery sticks or with natural, low salt corn chips.

Take off!

As well as good food, we also need to exercise to keep us fit. Exercise isn't just for our bodies. It does wonders for our brains as well, by helping to keep us alert and focused through the day. And it helps us to sleep soundly at night.

Why our bodies love exercise

Exercise does many things for us. It moves blood around our bodies. Blood carries **oxygen** and nutrients (from the food we eat), and delivers these to our bones and muscles. Exercise strengthens our lungs, heart, bones and muscles – all of which keeps us fit and gives us more energy.

Try to find an exercise that you enjoy doing.

Exercise also helps to keep us **coordinated**. The more exercise we do, the better we get at activities like throwing, catching and balancing. Being fitter and moving more helps to stop us from putting on too much weight, which can lead to health problems. Exercise also helps to boost our immune system, which is a part of the body that fights disease.

Mind and mood

Exercise carries oxygen to our brains. This helps us to think more clearly and stay focused. Exercise also helps us to sleep better, which is also good for our brains. Scientists have found that exercise causes reactions in our bodies that make us feel better and more relaxed. This means that the more we exercise, the more happy and confident we feel. And that means we are less stressed and nervous.

Types of exercise

Exercise is anything that we do to move our bodies. We do lots of exercise each day without even thinking about it. This includes walking to school or playing around with friends. But it is also good to have a range of different exercises to do each day. These could include muscle- and bone-strengthening exercises and stretching. About three times a week we should add in **aerobic exercise** – exercise that makes us breathe hard and raises the heartbeat.

Walking or riding to school is a great way to add exercise to your day.

You can choose

You can choose to improve the way you feel by getting at least an hour of exercise every day. If you are not doing this already, there are lots of ways to sneak exercise into your life so that you will hardly even notice it!

Movement of any kind is good for you. Instead of taking the car to school, walk or ride your bike. Take the stairs rather than the lift. Cut back on TV or the computer and go out and play for an hour after school. Some good ways to get a workout are running, jumping, swimming, kicking a ball around the backyard and playing tennis against a wall.

And don't forget strength and stretching. Easy stretching exercises can be done anywhere and any time. Strength training can be as easy as helping to carry the shopping or lifting your own weight by doing push-ups or chin-ups.

Stretch gently and slowly four or five times.

Fun moves

If you like playing sport, it's easy to get enough exercise. But lots of people don't like sport, so what happens then? It's easy to add in a walk or a bike-ride here and there, but sometimes it's difficult to add in a harder workout.

Did you know?
The more of any exercise you do, the better you get at it. So, even if you don't like doing something, if you keep doing it and practising as much as you can, you will improve!

A fun way to raise a sweat is to take a dance class. Or if you don't want to take a class you can put on your favourite music and dance at home. You can also make up your own dance moves. In the meantime, here are some simple moves to start you off.

Dance moves

Do each of these for ten seconds and repeat all of them ten times.

1 Let your body go loose, then shake all over.

2 Run on the spot.

3 Pretend you are riding a horse.

4 Do some star jumps.

Stay safe

Staying healthy and well means eating well and exercising, but it also means staying safe. This means looking after ourselves when we are in places like the beach, near the road or even in the playground. It also means being aware of the people around us and how they behave. We should also look out for other people who may need help. A large part of staying safe is planning how to deal with different **environments** and situations.

What does it mean to be safe?

Sometimes we know when we are not safe. We know because we feel a little frightened. At other times we might not realise something is unsafe until it's too late. Part of growing up is learning to work out how to avoid unsafe places and activities. Stop, think and plan – and listen to yourself. If you feel uneasy about something, there's probably a good reason. And remember, always talk to an adult you know and trust for help or advice.

It's important to be safe at all times in the playground.

Environmental safety

Environmental safety means being safe in a particular place or area. Some of the places we need to look out for the safety of ourselves and others include when we are:

- in the sun for a long time
- around water
- on or near roads
- in the playground
- in the kitchen or the bathroom.

Personal safety

Personal safety means looking out for ourselves around other people. Meeting new people is fun, but we always need to be careful. When online, personal safety is really important. Make sure an adult is aware of what you are doing and never share personal information with people you don't know. Personal safety also includes protecting yourself against bullying or feeling under pressure by friends to do things you don't feel happy about. It can also mean looking out for others who are being bullied.

It's important to feel safe wherever you are.

You can choose

Being prepared for different environments gives you more choices. Think about where you are going and what you are doing. Make a safety checklist. If you are going out in the sun be sure to wear a hat and a long-sleeved light shirt, use sunscreen and carry a big bottle of water. Knowing how to keep yourself safe in the sun means you can stay out for longer without getting sunburnt or **dehydrated**.

Did you know?

Our bodies are made up of about 60 per cent water! To stop getting dehydrated we need to drink about eight glasses of water to replace what we lose every day.

Sunscreen and a hat will help you stay safe from the sun.

Have a plan to deal with uncomfortable situations with other people. When you are out, always stay close to your friends and family. Never go anywhere with someone you don't know. Don't be afraid to yell out if you don't like what someone is doing.

Pedestrian traffic safety checklist

Traffic safety is important when you are walking across the road, and even when you are on a footpath. Always keep a look out for cars, bicycles and other **pedestrians**.

Remember to:

1 Always cross the road with an adult. If you are under eight years old, hold the adult's hand.

2 Whenever possible, cross the road at a pedestrian crossing. Cross only when you can see the 'green person' light up.

3 Even if you are on a pedestrian crossing, always check both ways for cars (right, then left, then right again). Look and listen.

4 Take care crossing side streets, carpark entrances and driveways. Check to see if there are any cars coming in or going out. Wait until the cars have passed before you walk on.

5 Always look out for bicycles, too. And be very careful if you are using a shared footpath and bicycle track. Keep to the left.

Take care when crossing the road.

Check it out!

As we get older we start to spend more time with our friends, and sometimes with people we don't know very well. At times it can be difficult being in new situations. This is especially true if people offer us substances. These can be things like food and drinks or tablets and medicines that we don't recognise. Or they might be things we think may be bad for our health or wellbeing.

Is that a drug?

Drugs are substances that can affect the brain or body. These include **alcohol** and **tobacco** (cigarettes). Others include painkillers and **prescription medicines**. Even herbs and drinks like tea and coffee count as drugs. Some drugs are stronger than others, but all have the power to harm us, especially if we take too much. Many drugs can help people who are sick – like painkillers or drugs for diseases. But even these drugs can be dangerous if we take too much of them, or take them when they are not meant for us.

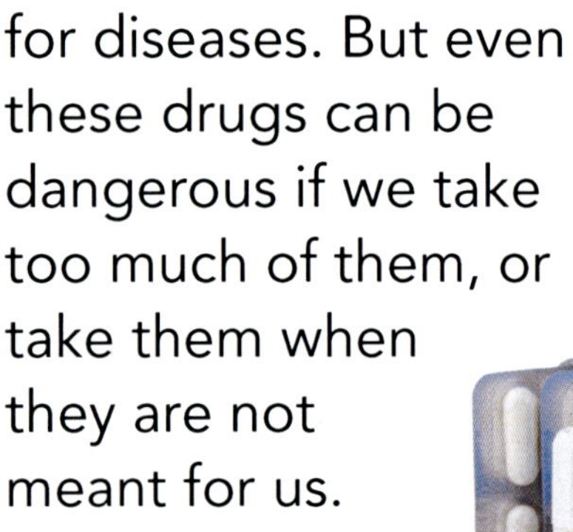

There are many different types of drugs.

Tea and coffee contain caffeine.

Everyday drugs

Even some everyday substances can contain drugs. Tea, coffee and energy drinks contain a drug called **caffeine**. Caffeine affects our **nervous system** and makes us more alert. It also makes us more irritable, nervous, can stop us from sleeping and can affect our hearts. While most adults can have a little bit of caffeine, it should not be taken by children. Although it is not a strong drug, some people can become very unwell from caffeine, especially those with heart problems.

Medicines

Medicines are drugs that are taken by people to treat illness or pain. Many of these are prescribed by doctors or other healthcare workers for their patients. It is important not to take medicine that has been prescribed for someone else. Medicines can act like poisons if they are not right for you. It is important that medicines are stored in a locked cupboard that can only be reached by an adult.

You can choose

Knowing more about drugs can help you to make choices. Find out what different drugs can do to your body – how they can affect you and how they can harm you. For example, alcohol not only affects people when they drink it, it can have long-term effects. Young people who drink alcohol can suffer from memory and learning problems for the rest of their lives.

And remember, be careful even if someone offers you something as simple as a tablet for a headache. Don't take it unless you check with a doctor, chemist or your parents first. If you do have a headache, try lying down quietly for a while or massage your head. The pain might go away without you having to take anything at all.

Did you know?

Lying quietly and breathing deeply for a few minutes can help you relax. This is not only good for headaches, but it is also good for your general health and wellbeing.

Rest is a good way to cure a headache.

What can you do?

What would you say or do if someone offered you a drug? Here are a few different ways you could possibly deal with that situation.

1 Say: "No thanks. I don't want to take something that will harm me or make me sick."
2 If the person still wants you to take something, tell them what is wrong with the drug they are offering. Explain the ways in which this drug can harm people who take it.
3 If they are offering you alcohol or tobacco, tell them what they are doing is illegal.
4 Walk away from the person and tell an adult who you know and trust what has happened.
5 Try to avoid people who might try to give you drugs. If you find yourself in an uncomfortable situation, try and leave as soon as possible.

Never be afraid to say 'No'.

Connections

Staying fit, healthy and happy can be hard work sometimes. But it's worth it. By eating well, exercising and staying safe from harm you will keep your body and mind in tip-top condition. If you try to stay healthy and feel good now it will set you up for the rest of your life.

Learning about healthy behaviours gives you more control over your life. It also gives you a lot of choices about how you can stay fit and well. As you grow up you can begin to make your own decisions about what is best for you. Knowing how to get information and use it to make positive choices is a skill you can keep on using all your life.

Staying fit, healthy and happy is worth it!

Glossary

aerobic exercise exercise that increases the heart rate and breathing

alcohol intoxicating liquid drug that affects the nervous system. Helps people relax; overuse can cause illness, damage or death

caffeine drug in coffee and tea. Stimulates the nervous system and makes people more alert, but also irritable and anxious

carbohydrates substances used by the body to provide energy

coordinated working together in smooth combination

dehydrated when the body lacks water

environment the surroundings in which something happens

minerals substances the human body needs for good health

nervous system set of nerves that control the body's activities

nutrients substances that provide nourishment essential for life and growth

oxygen colourless, odourless gas that makes up a part of air and is essential to life

pedestrians people travelling on foot

prescription medicines medicines prescribed by a doctor for one particular person's health problem

protein an essential part of all living things, important for growth

substances particular kinds of matter or material

tobacco plant containing the drug nicotine, usually smoked as a cigarette

vitamins substances needed by the body for growth and health

Index